-THIS-
JOURNAL
Belongs
-TO-

IF FOUND PLEASE
CONTACT

·PS·

NO JUDGMENT. I'M DOING THE *Best* I CAN. THANK YOU.

·OR·

Yep, LOOK AT ALL THE COOL STUFF I DO.

Major GOALS

_____
_____
_____
_____
_____
_____
_____
_____
_____
_____
_____
_____
_____
_____
_____

Mini GOALS

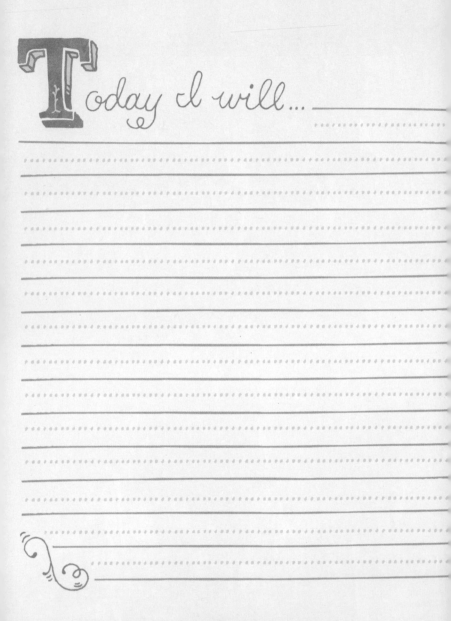

Today I will...

Feels

GOOD

TO GET SOME

Stuff Done

GUARANTEED

TODAY
= IS The DAY FOR... =

Have some

COFFEE

OR TEA

there's

WORK

to be

DONE

JUST Remember THE TITLE of this JOURNAL

WHY WAIT TILL Tomorrow?

MAKING *Lists* IS FUN!

Yesterday I was SUPPOSED to:

So, today I REALLY will...

go-getters are
Sexy!

I've
ALWAYS
wanted to

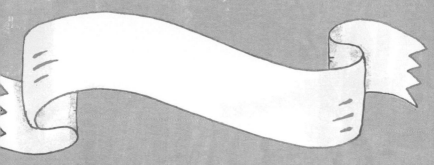

why not
TODAY?

WRITE a HAIKU!

IF TODAY goes well YOU MAY GO out for ICE CREAM

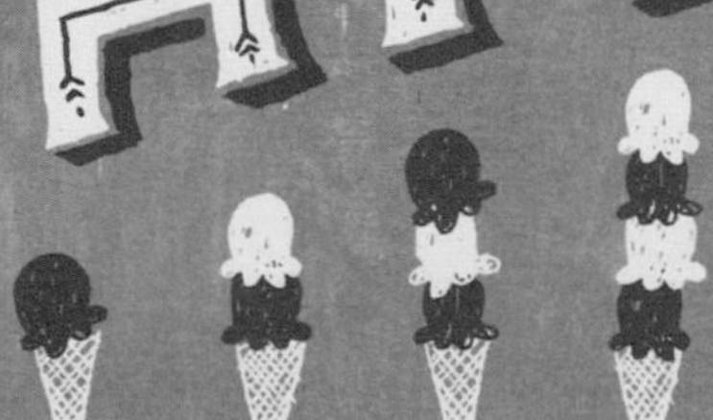

ISOLATED Thoughts

You deserve a Break

OKAY **BREAK'S** OVER!

Major GOALS

Mini GOALS

Today I will...

Feels
GOOD
TO GET SOME
Stuff Done
GUARANTEED

TODAY
= IS The DAY FOR... =

Have some

COFFEE

OR TEA

there's

WORK

to be

DONE

JUST Remember THE TITLE of this JOURNAL

WHY WAIT TILL Tomorrow?

MAKING *Lists* IS FUN!

Yesterday I was SUPPOSED to

So, today I REALLY will...

go-getters are
Sexy!

I've
ALWAYS
wanted to

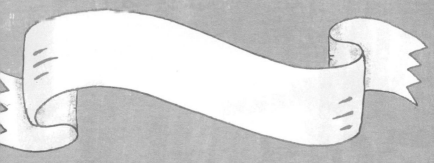

why not
TODAY?

WRITE a HAIKU!

IF TODAY goes well YOU MAY GO out for ICE CREAM

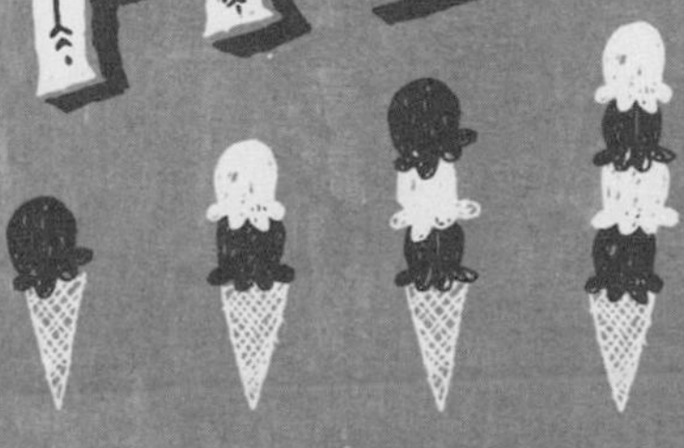

ISOLATED

Thoughts

You deserve a Break

OKAY **BREAK'S** OVER!

Major GOALS

Mini GOALS

Today I will...

Feels

GOOD

TO GET SOME

Stuff Done

GUARANTEED

TODAY

= IS The DAY FOR... =

Have some
COFFEE
OR TEA

there's

WORK
to be
DONE

JUST Remember THE TITLE of this JOURNAL

WHY WAIT TILL Tomorrow?

MAKING *Lists* IS FUN!

_____

_____

_____

_____

_____

_____

_____

_____

_____

_____

_____

_____

_____

_____

_____

_____

_____

_____

_____

_____

_____

_____

_____

_____

_____

_____

_____

_____

Yesterday I was SUPPOSED to

So, today I REALLY will...

---

go-getters are

Sexy!

I've ALWAYS wanted to

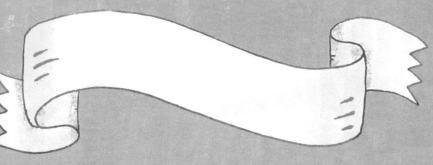

why not TODAY?

WRITE a HAIKU!

IF TODAY goes well YOU MAY GO out for ICE CREAM

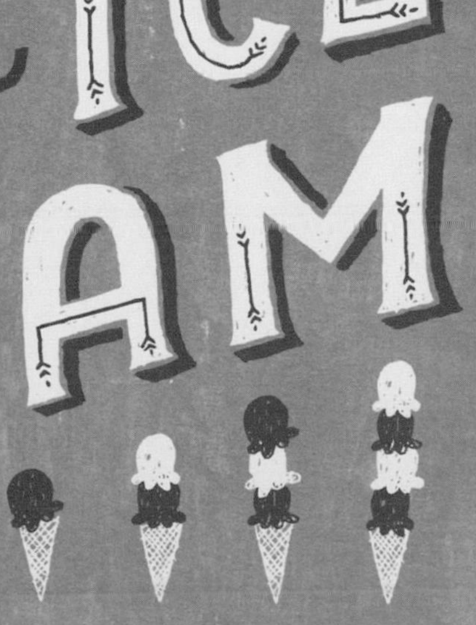

ISOLATED *Thoughts*

You deserve a Break

OKAY **BREAK'S** OVER!

Major GOALS

_____
_____
_____
_____
_____
_____
_____
_____
_____
_____
_____
_____
_____
_____
_____
_____

Mini GOALS

Today I will...

Feels

GOOD

TO GET SOME

Stuff Done

GUARANTEED

Have some
COFFEE
OR TEA
there's
WORK
to be
DONE

JUST Remember THE TITLE of this JOURNAL

WHY WAIT TILL *Tomorrow?*

MAKING *Lists* IS FUN!

Yesterday I was SUPPOSED to

So, today I REALLY will...

_____

_____

_____

_____

_____

_____

_____

_____

_____

_____

go-getters are
sexy!

I've

ALWAYS

wanted to

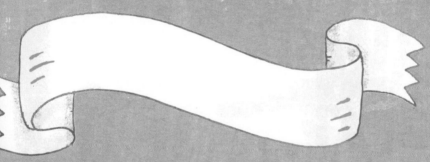

why not

TODAY?

WRITE a HAIKU!

IF TODAY goes well YOU MAY GO out for ICE CREAM

ISOLATED
Thoughts

You deserve a Break

OKAY **BREAK'S** OVER!

Major GOALS

Mini GOALS

Today I will..._____

Feels GOOD

TO GET SOME

Stuff Done

GUARANTEED

TODAY
= IS The DAY FOR... =

Have some

COFFEE

OR TEA

there's

WORK

to be

DONE

JUST Remember THE TITLE of this JOURNAL